PRAYER SIMPLIFIED!

PRAYER
SIMPLIFIED!

INSIGHTS INTO THE WHY,
THE WHAT, THE HOW &
THE WHEN OF PRAYER.

Toyin John

Unless otherwise stated, all Scriptural quotations are from the New King James Version of the Holy Bible.

ISBN: 978-0-9969117-1-9

Library of Congress Control Number: 2017944332

Published in Irvine, California by Giant Within Publishing House

First Printed in the United States of America.

CONTENTS

ACKNOWLEDGMENTS

A big thank you to my "one of a kind" husband, Emmanuel B. John for who you are to me and for your input in this work, you are the best. To my lovely children, Tami, Toni and Damilola, praying for and with you makes life really exciting.

A huge appreciation to my amazing parents, late Mr E.O Ajayi & Mrs Esther Ajayi, my wonderful spiritual parents, Rev Kola & Rev Funke Ewuosho, my loving Senior Pastors, Pastor Troy & Pastor Lori Perry, my power-filled PUSH Prayer Movement Global Family, all my dependable praying friends and countless anointed Ministers of the Gospel, my life has been greatly impacted by you all, my "Thank Yous" are endless.

DEDICATION

To the One who is my Life and Breath, my Lord and Savior Jesus Christ, through whom I have seen impossibilities made possible, this book is dedicated.

INTRODUCTION

Prayer has always been an important part of my life ever since I was a very young believer. I have seen the Lord move in my life in various ways and in the lives of others as a result of prayer. I have developed an enriching and intimate relationship with the Lord by relating with Him.

I always still feel a need to know more about prayer and how my prayer life can be more effective. I also derive a lot of joy in sharing with others, what I have learnt over the years.

This book was written to share some of those insights, it will introduce new believers to the concept of prayer and equip them. It will also enlighten other believers who long to know more about prayer.

I encourage you to read this book with an open mind, there is much more to learn about prayer not written here, but this can add to what you already *know or give you a fresh perspective into some aspects of prayer.*

All scriptures are from the New King James Version of the Bible except otherwise specified.

It is my sincere desire that, you will be greatly blessed and your prayer life enriched. My hope is that, you will immediately begin to practice whatever the Holy Spirit will teach you through this book.

Happy Reading!

One

Why is Prayer Important?

1

WHY IS PRAYER IMPORTANT?

I believe that before we can know why prayer is important, we need to first understand what prayer is. In an attempt to define what prayer is, different people have described what they understand by prayer, but one common thing that rings through several definitions is that, prayer is a way of man conversing with God.

In order to have a conversation, there has to be at least two people involved, so in the case of prayer, it is primarily a communication between man and God. It is meant to be a two-way exercise where both speaking and listening are actively taking place.

Prayer is important in the life of a believer because it is the very life-line of a believer's relationship with God, it connects us to our Source. The more effective a believer's prayer life is, the more effective his/her relationship with God will be.

Throughout the Bible, we will see the men of old engaging God in conversations because their very lives depended on it. Before the fall of man, God would fellowship with Adam and Eve in the Garden of Eden. But after the fall of man, the first mention of human beings calling on God was recorded when Enosh was born.

Genesis 4:26 (AMP) says: *"To Seth, also a son was born, whom he named Enosh (mortal man, mankind). At that (same) time men began to call on the name of the Lord (in worship through prayer, praise and thanksgiving)."*

God made provision for man to be able to call on Him, why? Because He is our Source and our lives are sustained by Him. If we truly grasp a hold of this understanding, prayer will not be a thing of drudgery as many have deemed it to be. A believer who is not connected to his/her Source is like someone who is walking with no life. Some of the patriarchs of old knew this secret and lived it.

Abraham the father of faith, prayed to God all the time. He interceded for Sodom and Gomorrah, it is believed, it was for the sake of his nephew, Lot, who lived in the city at the time with his family (Genesis 18:23-33). Though the city was destroyed, Abraham's nephew was saved. God referred to Abraham as a friend and shared secrets of what would happen with him. This could only have happened because a relationship had been built through communication.

David walked with the Lord, he was called the man after God's heart, he went through a lot before he finally became king and even afterward. He was in constant communication with God as displayed in the scriptures especially the Psalms, he knew the secret of being in God's presence, connected to Him, receiving strength every step of the way.

The Lord Jesus Christ who is the Author and Finisher of our faith, prayed all the time. Matthew 14:23: *"And when He had sent the multitudes away, he went up on the mountain by Himself to pray. Now when evening came, He was alone there."*

Mark 1:35: *"Now in the morning, having risen a long while before daylight, He went out and departed to a solitary place; and there He prayed."*

Why did He have to pray since He Himself was divine? He had to because He was also fully Man and He knew that in order for Him to carry out the will of the Father, He must stay connected to Him, He must pray! He said in John 5:19: *"Then Jesus answered and said to them, 'Most assuredly, I say to you, the Son can do nothing of Himself, but what He sees the Father do; for whatever He does, the Son also does in like manner.'"*

He is our ultimate example of what our relationship with God ought to be and if we must live purposefully, we must stay plugged in to the Source. If we must carry out God's will for our lives, we must be in constant communication with the One who made and sent us. We must pray!

Prayer

Dear heavenly Father, I am so thankful to be called Your very own. Thank You for making a way for me to have a relationship with You through the death, burial and resurrection of my Lord and Savior Jesus Christ.

Lord Jesus, thank You for paying the ultimate sacrifice for me to be redeemed, I am free to worship and serve God with my being. Holy Spirit, thank You for being my Guide, my Teacher and my Advocate. Thank You for showing me how to develop my relationship with the Lord Jesus, thank You for teaching me the word of God and guiding me to live a life that pleases God.

I declare that, I am a child of the living God, His life is in me. I am an overcomer through Christ Jesus, who died for my sins and was raised for my justification, through whom, my eternity is secure. I thank You that You hear me always in Jesus' name. Amen.

NOTES

Two

The Art of Prayer

2

THE ART OF PRAYER

While prayer is a way of communicating with God and it is essential to our existence as believers on this earth, we must know how to pray.

The disciples of the Lord Jesus, after having been with Him for some time and obviously, must have observed that He was always going away alone just to pray, asked Him to teach them how to pray (Luke 11:1).

There are many teachings on the art of prayer and many great books have been written to touch on the subject. For the purpose of this study, we will look into how the Lord Jesus taught His disciples to pray.

Matthew 6:9-13: "In this manner, therefore, pray:

9.   Our Father in heaven, hallowed be Your name.

10. *Your Kingdom come. Your will be done on earth as it is in heaven.*

11. *Give us this day our daily bread.*

12. *And forgive us our debts, as we forgive our debtors.*

13. *And do not lead us into temptation but deliver us from the evil one. For Yours is the kingdom and the power and the glory forever. Amen."*

Even though the above is an outline of the "how to pray" the Lord Jesus taught His disciples, and this has been literally recited as it is in some Christian circles, I truly believe that, it shows us the basis on which we can approach God in prayer. Many great Bible teachers have taught on this as well.

Matthew 6:9 shows us how to approach God in reverence because He is worthy of our praise and adoration. Psalm 100:4 says: *"Enter into His gates with thanksgiving and into His courts with praise. Be thankful to Him and bless His name."* This is the way we ought to come before Him, giving Him thanks, honoring His name in adoration. He is our Father, we are His children and we ought to approach Him in a relational way rather than, a mechanical way. Give Him praise and worship Him in the beauty of His holiness.

This is where we minister to Him, lost in His presence, declaring our love for Him and even singing songs of worship and adoration to Him, in acknowledgment of who He is, in our lives.

Matthew 6:10 summons us to superimpose His kingdom and His will over every situation. This is a place of surrender, where we acknowledge His will in our lives and whatever we are praying for.

Matthew 6:11 lets us know we can make our requests known to Him. The Bible says that, God daily loads us with benefits (Psalm 68:19). We can intercede for others as well, for the needs in their lives to be met.

Matthew 6:12 teaches us about an important aspect of prayer which is forgiveness, we receive forgiveness from God as we give forgiveness to others. The Lord Jesus stressed this point in verses 14&15 of Matthew 6 saying: *"For if you forgive men their trespasses, your heavenly Father will also forgive you. 15. But if you do not forgive men their trespasses, neither will your heavenly Father forgive your trespasses."* It is essential to pause and think on this point very well because many prayers have been hindered due to unforgiveness. This is expounded on, in one of the chapters in this book.

Matthew 6:13a lets us know that, we ought to depend on God for His grace not to fall into temptation, also to rely on His deliverance and protection from the enemy. Temptation in that context, means trials and tests. The devil is the enemy of God's children and he is constantly scheming. This is the reason the Bible admonishes us to be; *"sober and vigilant"* (1Peter 5:8). Thank God! Greater is He that is in us, than the devil that is in the world.

Matthew 6:13b shows us how to end our time of prayer, in worship and adoration of the Father, acknowledging His sovereignty, giving Him glory.

As we progress in an active walk with God, this becomes a part of our lives and it develops as we know Him more, and dig deeper in our relationship with Him.

As much as it is important to talk to Him, it is important to also listen intently to Him. That is why it is a two-way communication. When you finish praying, you may want to maintain a period of silence while still in that attitude of prayer. He may speak to you as you study His word. He may lead you to do something you were not thinking before, it may come as a prompting or an urge within you from the Holy Spirit, and when you act on that prompting, you will see results (Romans 8:14).

People have argued; how do I really know it is God speaking to me or is it just my mind or even the devil? Deciphering the voice of God develops as you grow deeper in Him, the more you get to know Him, the clearer His voice gets and the better you know it.

Whatever He tells you will not contradict His word, this is a primary thing you want to learn about when He speaks to you. He also will not strive, the Holy Spirit is gentle, He will not impose on you but as you learn to listen, you will surely be able to know His voice when He speaks to you (John 10:27).

It is important to know that, if you set a regular time to pray in the morning and you use the "how to" as taught by our Lord Jesus Christ as explained here, that does not mean you cannot talk to Him again throughout the day. In actual fact, I encourage you to invite Him into your day, as you drive, as you go to work, as you go about your daily activities, let Him be a part of you throughout your day.

Some may argue that, you don't necessarily have to start your day with spending time in God's presence, I see this as a matter of priority.

Spending time with God first thing in the morning can set the tone for the rest of your day. You may have planned out a day but ultimately you do not necessarily know the surprises that life may spring up on you. But God knows because He is Omniscient. If you cultivate spending quality time with Him first thing in the morning, He will guide your paths throughout the day. If you stay connected to Him and sensitive to His Holy Spirit, you will not fall into the enemy's traps.

The Lord Jesus prayed through the night and early in the morning as well. Mark 1:35 says: *"Now in the morning, having risen a long while before daylight, He went out and departed to a solitary place; and there He prayed."* It makes sense to start one's day in God's presence while staying connected with Him the entire day. Invite Him into every area of your life, talk to him like a friend, you'll be amazed at how easy it is to relate with Him.

I involve Him in my life because He loves to be involved. I often ask Him to help me find parking spots. I remember having a tough situation with my hair, and I needed a way out that would take all the burden I had at the time regarding my hair. I often spoke to the Lord about it and it is amazing to say that, He heard each time till He led me to the final decision I made with my hair, which has been the best so far. I mean something as insignificant as my hair, He got involved and gave me a solution because I let Him in. God cares about every detail of our lives but we must be willing to invite and allow Him in.

The enemy is cheating a lot of believers from enjoying the fullness of God, by making prayer feel like a mechanical action they have to perform, rather than a beautiful part of an intimate relationship with a loving God.

Prayer

Dear Lord Jesus, thank You for showing me the way to the Father. Thank You for teaching me how to pray. I praise Your mighty name and I worship You for who You are.

I declare that Your kingdom comes upon my life, the lives of my loved ones, Your Church and my nation, in righteousness, peace and joy in the Holy Ghost. I declare Your will over every situation and according to Your word, let Your counsel alone stand in everything.

Lord, You are my Source of total supply and I shall not lack for anything, all my needs are met according to Your riches in glory by Christ Jesus. Deliver me from every trial and tribulation that the enemy may throw my way, I claim divine protection over every ability of the devil. I declare that, no evil shall befall me and my loved ones, neither shall any plague come near our dwelling places in Jesus'name.

Lord, I forgive and release everyone that has hurt me in one way or another as I receive total forgiveness of my own shortcomings from You.

I praise Your Holy name for You are worthy and all power, honor and glory are yours. I thank You because I know You have heard me. In Jesus' name I pray, Amen.

NOTES

Three

Different Types of Prayer

3

DIFFERENT TYPES OF PRAYER

While prayer is communicating with God, as a believer, you must know that, there are different types of prayer as well. It is important to engage the right kind of prayer in the right situation.

Every other type of prayer is built on our relationship with God. Nothing can take the place of you fellowshipping with God on a daily basis, cultivating being in His presence every time. I truly believe that, the essence of our Christian walk, flows from our intimacy with God. Having said these things, let's examine some of the different types of prayer and how they were used in the Bible.

a. The Prayer of Praise and Thanksgiving

As earlier mentioned, it is note-worthy to say that, we ought to approach God with praise and thanksgiving when we come into His presence. Psalm 100:4 says: *"Enter His gates with thanksgiving, and His courts with praise. Be thankful to Him and bless His name."* This should be a part of us, flowing out of our very being every time we go before Him. There are times, when God answers prayers with physical manifestations, or He does something great, prayer of praise and thanksgiving comes into play as well.

This is evident throughout the Bible. Mary the mother of our Lord Jesus Christ exhibited this prayer of praise after she was divinely visited by the angel. Luke 1:46-55 describes how she let out a prayer of praise and adoration to honor God.

Prayer of praise and thanksgiving should be woven into the fabric of our lives. It indicates that, we acknowledge God's mercy over us and we see it as a mighty privilege. It is our way of honoring Him. The Bible lets us know that, when we offer praises to God, we prepare the way for Him to show us His salvation (Psalm 50:23) (Lamentations 3:22-24).

b. The Prayer of Agreement

A prayer of agreement is when two or more people come together in prayer, to agree on what the word of God says, concerning a particular situation. It is important to also know that, a believer can join together with God to agree with Him on His word.

Our Lord Jesus showed us how powerful the prayer of agreement can be in Matthew 18:19: *"Again I say to you that, if two of you agree on earth concerning anything that they ask, it will be done for them by My Father in heaven."*

In order for the prayer of agreement to be effective, the two parties must be in complete agreement about what they want to pray about.

The Disciples of Christ prayed when they were persecuted and because they were in agreement, they witnessed the power of God, Acts 4:24: *"So when they heard that, they raised their voice to God with one accord and said"*........ "One accord" here, indicates agreement. Vs 31 of the same chapter says: *"And when they had prayed, the place where they were assembled together was shaken; and they were all filled with the Holy Spirit and they spoke the word of God with boldness."*

Prayer of agreement is powerful because a lot can be accomplished when people come together in agreement to pray, in accordance with God's will. The disciples of Christ knew this too well and did it often. Joining your faith with someone else in agreement gets results!

Deuteronomy 32:30 (NIV) says: *"How could one man chase a thousand or two put ten thousand to flight, unless their Rock had sold them, and the Lord had given them up?"* God can achieve many mighty things on earth when believers come together in agreement to pray.

c. The Prayer of faith

In order to engage in the prayer of faith, the believer has to understand what faith is. The Bible says in Hebrews 11:1 (AMP): *"Now faith is the title deed, confirmation of things hoped for (divinely guaranteed), and the evidence of things not seen (the conviction of their reality —faith comprehends as*

35

fact what cannot be experienced by the physical senses)." Faith is simply agreeing with what God says. You may not see it with your physical eyes, but, you deem Him who said it, faithful to keep His word and bring what He has said to pass. You believe in your heart before you see it, not when you see it.

Jesus said in Mark 11:24: *"Therefore I say to you, whatever things you ask when you pray, believe that you receive them, and you will have them."* If you look at this scripture very well, Christ is telling us to **BELIEVE** that, we **RECEIVE** whatever our requests are **WHEN** we pray, and it is after then, we will **HAVE** them. This is the reason why this is called the prayer of faith, because the believing comes first. Faith contradicts your physical senses, you must tap into your spirit to activate faith. One man of God described faith as a mystery.

However it is important to know that, whatever we are asking for must be in line with God's will for our lives because He will not go against His own will. How we can help ourselves is by aligning our will with

36

His, so that, we can experience His mighty hand in our situations. His will is His word, we can know His will when we clearly know what His word says concerning our situations. Many believers are not receiving answers to their prayers, partly because they are not praying in line with God's will concerning the situation.

Prayer of faith with corresponding action will bring to pass breakthroughs in the life of a believer that will do it. Many people received miracles from the Lord Jesus simply because they had faith in Him and acted on it. Matthew 15:21-38 tells us the story of the Canaanite woman, who would not take no for an answer until her daughter was healed. In verse 28 the Lord Jesus told her: *"O woman, great is your faith! Let it be to you as you desire."*

The Bible records in the latter part of that verse that her daughter was healed from that very hour. She had faith that Jesus was able to heal her daughter, she made a move to approach Him and relentlessly stood on that platform of faith and would not get off till she got what she asked for. Faith always moves the hand of God!

The woman with the issue of blood in Luke 8:43-48, thought to herself that, if she could but touch the hem of the garment of Christ, she would be made whole and that was exactly what she experienced. She had faith in Him, then acted on that faith by approaching the Lord, to get a hold of His garment against all odds. The Lord Jesus Christ affirmed this by saying to her in Luke 8:48: *"Daughter, be of good cheer; your faith has made you well. Go in peace."* She experienced her miracle because she acted on her faith.

d. The Prayer of Intercession

Intercession is the act of intervening on behalf of another person. The prayer of intercession is when you go before God on behalf of someone else. We see this in operation throughout the Bible. In Genesis 18:16-33, Abraham interceded for Sodom and Gomorrah for the sake of Lot, his nephew. Moses interceded several times on behalf of the children of Israel (Exodus

32:30-33; Deuteronomy 9: 13-19). The early believers interceded on behalf of Peter when he was imprisoned by Herod (Acts 12:5). The Lord Jesus Christ is interceding for us (Romans 8:34).

You and I can also take advantage of this privilege and intercede on behalf of our nations, the Body of Christ, our loved ones and others. When we stand in the gap for others in accordance with God's word, we invite heaven to bear upon their situations. There may be people in your life who are not in any position to pray, it may be due to their situation or they are lost, weak, helpless or simply not believers, you can stand in the gap for them in prayer, inviting God to the scenes of their lives.

e. The Prayer of Consecration

To consecrate is to set oneself apart from anything that can contaminate one's relationship with God. God is a holy God and it must be our desire to want to separate ourselves for His use.

The Lord instructed Moses to consecrate the children of Israel and get them ready to meet God (Exodus 19:10-11).

Joshua also asked the children of Israel to consecrate themselves in preparation to experience God's wonders (Joshua 3:5). King David prayed a prayer of consecration in Psalm 51 after his sin was confronted.

God is holy and God wants us to be holy. The Bible says in 1Peter 1:15-16: *"but as He who called you is holy, you also be holy in all your conduct, because it is written, "Be holy, for I am holy."*

We pray the prayer of consecration with the awareness that, our God wants us separated unto Him. The Bible says in 2 Corinthians 6:17: *"Therefore, Come out from among them and be separate, says the Lord. Do not touch what is unclean, and I will receive you."*

The Lord wants us as believers to set ourselves apart for Him, we may live in this world but the world does not have to live in us. It may sound impossible to some people that, as believers we can consecrate ourselves to the extent that, the world will no longer have an effect on us. The truth is, it is possible, God will not ask us to do what He has not given us the ability to do, His grace is available to help us.

I believe that, part of our consecration is to embrace a consciousness of living intentionally, dedicated for God's use. Romans 12:1-2 says: *"I beseech you therefore, brethren, by the mercies of God, that you present your bodies a living sacrifice, holy, acceptable to God, which is your reasonable service." 2. "And do not be conformed to this world, but be transformed by the renewing of your mind, that you may approve what is that good and acceptable and perfect will of God."*

The Bible actually says to present our bodies as a living sacrifice...is our reasonable service. It is evident that, consecration must be part of our daily walk with God.

It is important to note this; there is nothing we can do to buy God's love, His love for us is unconditional. But if we love Him, we will set ourselves apart for Him. John 14:15 says: *"If ye love Me, keep My commandments."*

f. The Warfare Prayer

God is a Spirit, and He lives in the invisible world which we cannot see nor touch physically (John 4:24). Man lives in a physical world, which we can see, feel and touch with our senses. The spirit/invisible world, controls the physical/visible world. Hebrews 11:3 (CEB) says: *"By faith we understand that the universe has been created by a word from God so that the visible came into existence from the invisible."*

Unfortunately, not many people are aware of this, and many that are aware of this, do not know how to deal with this other world. Only a few know the dynamics of how things work in the realm of the spirit/the invisible realm. The good news is that, God has not left us without a solution, Christ stripped the enemy of his powers when He came to this earth. He said in Luke 10:19: *" Behold, I give you the authority to trample on serpents and scorpions and over all the power of the enemy, and nothing shall by any means hurt you."*

Now, the act of exercising that authority over the abilities of the enemy is the warfare prayer. Matthew 18:18 says: *"Assuredly, I say to you, whatever you bind on earth will be bound in heaven, and whatever you loose on earth will be loosed in heaven."* We are not to be afraid of the enemy but, we being in right standing with God, are supposed to put him in his place and take authority over every one of his operations.

Prayer

Dear God, thank You for the authority I have in Christ Jesus over every ability of the enemy. Today, I pull down every stronghold, I cast down every argument and every high thing that has exalted itself above the knowledge of God in my mind. I bring every thought into captivity to the obedience of Christ.

I declare that, I have the mind of Christ therefore, my mind is clear, sound and wise. Fear, defeat, doubt and unbelief have no hold over me. I plead the blood of Jesus over my spirit, soul and body. My steps are guided by the Holy Spirit and He leads me in the way of everlasting life. I give You praise for in Jesus' name I pray, Amen.

NOTES

Four

A prayerful Christian is a Powerful Christian

4

A PRAYERFUL CHRISTIAN IS A POWERFUL CHRISTIAN

There is a popular saying that says that: "A prayerless Christian is a powerless Christian." The Bible says in Ephesians 6:12: *"For we do not wrestle against flesh and blood, but against principalities, against powers, against the rulers of the darkness of this age, against spiritual hosts of wickedness in the heavenly places."* How exactly do we wrestle with these? It's in prayer. The word of God in the name of Jesus, is the weapon we use in prayer to defeat the enemy. It is not whining and complaining, it is heartfelt fervent BOLD prayer, the type that gets heaven's attention and destroys the plans of the enemy.

Daniel discovered a prophecy and based on that discovery, he went into prayer coupled with fasting, to seek God's face and plead on behalf of his people. He stayed in that place of prayer and received a divine visitation from heaven (Daniel 9).

A believer must embrace prayer as a lifestyle, as much as it is our communication line with God, it is also the divine ability God has given us to experience victory on earth.

Throughout the Bible, the saints of old sought God's face in prayer and He answered them. Regardless of the situation, they called upon Him because that was what they had, and they experienced His hand.

Hannah was embittered in her soul because she was barren, and was taunted by her rival but she spoke to the Lord in prayer. 1 Samuel 1:10 says: *"And she was in bitterness of soul, and prayed to the Lord and wept in anguish".* And her prayer was answered. 1 Samuel 1:19-20: *Then they rose early in the morning and worshipped before the Lord, and returned and came to their house at Ramah. And Elkanah knew Hannah his wife, and the Lord remembered her."* 20. *"So it came to pass in the process of time that Hannah conceived and bore a son, and called his name Samuel, saying, 'Because I have asked for him from the Lord.'"* All she had against her situation and the oppression she faced was prayer and faith in a mighty God.

When the disciples were persecuted, beaten and threatened, they always came together to pray and received boldness to declare the word. They prayed to God in the name of Jesus, which is a mighty weapon in prayer (Acts 4:23-31).

When Peter was arrested to be killed by Herod, the believers came together in prayer to intercede on his behalf. They stayed in the place of prayer till he was released (Acts 12:5-10).

That same privilege of prayer is available to us too because the God we pray to, is well and alive. If we will pray and not faint (Luke 18:1), we will experience the hand of God.

Prayer

Dear Lord Jesus, I thank You for spoiling principalities and powers, making an open show of them, defeating the enemy and stripping him of all his powers.

I take authority over every force of darkness waging war against my destiny and your call upon my life. I speak to the dry places in my life to receive Your life and vitality.

I bind every spirit from hell that must have been sent in array against my soul and I render all their activities null, void and of no effect in the mighty Name of Jesus. Amen.

NOTES

Five

Power in the Name of Jesus

5

POWER IN THE NAME OF JESUS

As a believer of Jesus Christ, you must know the word of God to exercise your full authority in prayer. The Name of Jesus is powerful, demons tremble at His Name. Just before He left, He told His disciples the signs that would follow those who believe in Him; Mark 16:17-18 says: *"And these signs will follow those who believe: In My name they will cast out demons; they will speak with new tongues;" 18. "They will take up serpents; and if they drink anything deadly, it will by no means hurt them; they will lay hands on the sick and they will recover."* All these and much more in His Name! How is it done? In declaration and in prayer.

Christ is the center of our belief and it is by and through Him that we are victorious. The demons know this and they tremble. When the seven sons of Sceva tried to use that Name in a deceitful way, they were exposed by the same demon they were trying to cast out. (Acts 19:13-16). Even the demons knew who had the authority to use that Name.

While the Lord Jesus was on earth, the evil spirits recognized Him, the mere sight of Him tormented them (Luke 4:33-36; Matthew 8:28-34). Now that, He is no longer physically on earth, He is alive in every believer that has accepted Him as their Lord and Savior and because of this, they have the power to exercise authority in His Name. He said, greater works that He did while on earth, shall we do as believers. John 14:12-14 says: *"Most assuredly, I say to you, he who believes in Me, the works that I do he will do also; and greater works than these he will do, because I go to my Father." 13. "And whatever you ask in My name, that I will do, that the Father may be glorified in the Son." 14. "If you ask anything in My name, I will do it."*

Through the mighty name of Jesus, a person can experience healing, deliverance, breakthroughs, liberty and so on and so forth. The Holy Spirit was sent to us in the name of Jesus and through the same Name, He is received to teach us all things (John 14:26).

It is important to know that, without Christ, there is no Christianity, therefore faith in His name is the anchor of our salvation. This is the reason why, it is absolutely unacceptable to use that Name anyhow. Many people do so, they treat it with no gravity. How then can the Name work for them in prayer when it is already commonized?

His Name is above all names and it must be treated with all awe and reverence. Philippians 2:9-10 says: *"Therefore God has highly exalted Him and given Him the Name which is above every name, that at the Name of Jesus every knee should bow, of those in heaven, and of those on earth, and of those under the earth, and that every tongue should confess that Jesus Christ is Lord, to the glory of God the Father."*

Prayer

Dear Lord Jesus, I just want to thank You for the power in Your Holy Name. I appreciate You for giving me the right to exercise the authority in Your Name in any situation I may face in life.

I declare that, Your Name is my triumph over every tactic of the enemy and because of this, I am victorious. Thank You for the privilege I have in this powerful Name.

According to Your word, I run into Your Name and I am safe. I confess that, I am preserved from every calamity, hurt, harm, danger and tragedy, and I am forever protected. In Your mighty Name I pray. Amen.

NOTES

Six

Effects of Prayer in the Life of a Believer

6

EFFECTS OF PRAYER IN THE LIFE OF A BELIEVER

It is commonly said that: **"communication is to a relationship, as blood is to life."** If prayer is our way of communicating with God, then, it is the very heartbeat of our relationship with Him. Let's examine a few effects of prayer in the life of a believer.

1. **Closeness to God** – A believer of Christ that communicates with God regularly, will grow closer to Him and enjoy cultivating being in His presence as a lifestyle. There is an assurance coupled with indescribable peace and unspeakable joy that a believer can enjoy as a result of this (Psalm 145:18).

2. **Strong faith** – A praying Christian will grow in his or her faith as he/she spends time

with God daily. To know God is to know His word, and to know His word is to be able to grow your faith and pray effectively. They go hand in hand. Faith has a life of its own in the existence of a believer, the more you exercise your faith, the bigger and stronger it grows (Mark 11:23-24).

3. **Peace in the midst of storms** – Praying to God in the midst of difficulties, gives a believer peace and the confidence that God is in control and will work things out (Philippians 4:6-8).

4. **Hope** – In a world where there is so much hopelessness, it is comforting to know that, we as believers can have hope in God. Prayer makes us hopeful in all things. Hannah became hopeful after pouring her heart to God in prayer. She must have felt a relief that comes as a result of hope. The Bible records that, she ate and was no longer sad. At that moment, her physical circumstance had not changed but her heart became hopeful because she had met with God in prayer (1Samuel 1:18).

5. **Courage** – Prayer strengthens our hearts and gives us courage in the midst of trials because we know we are not alone. The Lord Jesus Christ prayed just before He was arrested, though He was weak and troubled, He agonized in prayer and was strengthened to fulfill God's will (Luke 22:41-43).

6. **Boldness** – Prayer gives the believer boldness to walk through the challenges of life and face oppositions. When the disciples of the Lord Jesus Christ were forbidden to preach in His name, they prayed and received boldness to continue, disregarding the threats against them (Acts 4:18 -31).

These are just some of the benefits of prayer, you will discover much more as you grow in your walk with God. I encourage you to live a prayerful life that is rooted in an intimate relationship with God, there is nothing compared to it.

Prayer

Dear Lord, I am grateful for knowing you. The ability to communicate with You in prayer, brings unspeakable joy to my soul.

I receive the spirit of wisdom and revelation in the knowledge of You. I declare that, the eyes of my heart are flooded with light and that I know the hope to which You have called me.

Grant unto me according to the riches of Your glory to be strengthened in my inner man with might by Your precious Holy Spirit.

I declare that, Christ dwells in my heart through faith, that, I am rooted and grounded in love and able to comprehend with all the saints the fullness of Your love.

Draw my heart close to You my God, and help me to know You more and more, in Jesus' name I pray.

Amen.

NOTES

Seven

The Roles of Prayer in the Fulfilment of Prophecy

7

THE ROLE OF PRAYER IN THE FULFILMENT OF PROPHECY

Prophecy is foretelling the future things to come. God foretold the coming of the Messiah through the mouths of His prophets even before the Messiah appeared on the scene. Isaiah 9: 6 says: *"For unto us a Child is born, unto us a Son is given: And the government will be upon His shoulder. And His name will be called Wonderful, Counselor, Mighty God, Everlasting Father, Prince of Peace."* This was prophet Isaiah prophesying the birth of the Lord Jesus Christ, years ahead of time.

However, the Bible introduced us to one of the saints, who was praying for the fulfilment of this prophecy. Luke 2:36-38 talks about prophetess Anna who served God with fastings and prayers, night and day. She recognized the Lord Jesus when He was brought into the temple, to be dedicated when He was just eight days old.

She spoke of the baby Jesus to all those who looked for redemption in Jerusalem. She knew about the prophecies of the coming Messiah and she was praying for years so when there was a manifestation, she recognized it and testified of it.

When Daniel read about the prophecy of Jeremiah regarding Israel, he went into prayer on behalf of his nation, to seek God's face for the fulfilment of the prophecy (Daniel 9). He received a divine encounter as previously mentioned.

The word of God is prophetic in nature but, it is important to know that, it must be birthed in prayer as well, in order to experience some divine manifestations.

Paul charged Timothy, his spiritual son to contend in prayer by the prophecies given to him, 1Timothy 1:18: *"This charge I commit to you, son Timothy, according to the prophecies previously made concerning you, that by them you may wage the good warfare."*

Any word of prophecy must line up with the word of God and with that, we as believers of Christ can take His word to Him in prayer. The Bible says in Isaiah 55:11: *"So shall My word be that goes forth from My mouth; It shall not return to Me void, but it shall accomplish what I please, and it shall prosper in the thing for which I sent it."*

Prayer

Dear God, thank You for the promises You have blessed me with, in Your word. I prophesy over every area of my life to flourish according to Your word. I declare that my steps are ordered by the Holy Spirit. I am led in the best pathway for my life according to Your divine purpose for me. I fulfill God's purpose for my life in Jesus' name, Amen.

NOTES

Eight

Prayer as a Foundation and Bedrock of any Work

8

PRAYER AS A FOUNDATION AND BEDROCK OF ANY WORK

The foundation of anything is important because it determines how the structure will be sustained on the long run. Jesus laid emphasis on building on a solid foundation in the word, (Matthew 7:24-27). A strong foundation will uphold the structure when storms come and a weak foundation will cause the structure to crumble.

It is important to know that staying in constant touch with God, seeking His face in prayer for guidance and direction, aligning our ways with His word, laying all our plans and desires before His throne and being willing to follow His lead no matter what, will give us a solid foundation to build on.

Seeking God's face in prayer lets you know the proper timing to do a thing and when to get out of another. Psalm 32:8 says: *"I will instruct you and teach you in the way you should go; I will guide you with My eye."* If we will pray the price, we will experience God's leading.

It is not enough to just lay a good foundation in prayer, it should be the bedrock of what you do, the pillar that holds it all together, the divine sustainability that the enemy cannot destroy. Will there be trials? Absolutely yes! Jesus says in John 16:33 that: *"These things I have spoken to you, that in Me you may have peace. In the world you will have tribulation; but be of good cheer, I have overcome the world."*

This shows clearly that, there will be tribulations but because we are in Him, we will have peace and because He has overcome the world, we are overcomers as well. But only those who are in touch with Him will experience this on a regular basis.

Developing a close relationship with God in prayer and His word will keep us intact, regardless of what may come our way. He will lead and guide us by His Spirit but we must be willing to listen to and obey His instructions.

The Bible says in Proverbs 10:25 (NLT): *"When the storms of life come, the wicked are whirled away, but the godly have a lasting foundation."* This scripture clearly shows that, the storms of life will come, it says: "when the storms of life come" not "if the storms of life come." The good news is that, the godly will have a lasting foundation. Why?

Because they built on Christ.

How do you build on a solid foundation? Through a rich and intimate relationship with God, in constant communication with Him in prayer, consistent study, meditation and practice of the word. Being planted in a Bible believing/teaching/practicing church will cause the believer to grow in his/her faith as well.

Believers that have these things in place, will survive the storms because their foundation is lasting. The question now is, are you building on a solid foundation? If not, it is not too late to start.

Prayer

Dear Heavenly Father, my heart pants after you, I long to know You more. Fill me with an ever increasing knowledge of who You are and cause me to continually dwell in Your presence all the days of my life.

Help me to build a foundation that is lasting. I receive the grace to stay the course in the race set for me.

Please help me not to deviate from the path of eternal life that You have me on and let be me a light to everyone that comes my way. I receive the grace to listen to and obey Your instructions. Help me to follow wherever You may lead me, I pray in the mighty name of Jesus.

NOTES

Nine

Jesus' Heart for Prayer

9

JESUS' HEART FOR PRAYER

There is no doubt that, the Lord Jesus lived a life of prayer when He was physically here on earth. Several Bible passages refer to Him withdrawing from the crowd to pray; Luke 5:16: *"So He Himself often withdrew into the wilderness and prayed."* He was fully God and He was fully human, yet He prayed. His life is an example to follow, the Bible says He was tempted in every way yet without sin (Hebrews 4:15). He did not become distracted or get carried away by the demands of this world that, He forgot to pray. He made it His lifestyle and it was apparent to those who followed Him closely.

The enemy came to test Him but could not prevail against Him because He was in touch with His Father, the Holy Spirit led and guided Him. He was in complete alignment with His Father's will. When His hour of sorrow drew near and His flesh became weak, He sought heaven in prayer and the angels attended to and strengthened Him (Luke 22:41-43).

He knew all things, nothing was created without Him, yet He prayed. Even now that, He is in heaven, the Bible says; He keeps on praying, making intercession for us (Romans 8:34).

For us to experience an end time harvest, the Lord Jesus clearly said that, we should pray for God to send laborers into the harvest field (Matthew 9:38).

When His disciples could not cast out a demon and asked him why they couldn't do so, He told them plainly that, cases like that one could only be dealt with, by prayer and fasting (Matthew 17:21).

All these show that, it is not enough to follow Him, nor is it enough to just attend church, in order to do some exploits, we must pray and in many cases fast as well.

He prayed for Peter so that, his faith would not fail because He knew he would betray Him (Luke 22:32). He charged His disciples to pray not to enter into temptation (Matthew 26:41). There are temptations all around us, enough trials to make one's faith waver but, when we stay connected to God through prayer and His word, we will overcome.

Jesus' heart for prayer is the full essence of a believer's relationship with God. He lived a life of prayer leaving us an example to follow. He did not only say it, He did it. As demanding as His work on earth was, He knew when to withdraw from the crowd to seek God's face in prayer. No wonder He only did what He saw the Father do (John 5:19).

If we must live victoriously as Christians, we must make time for prayer, we must be in touch with heaven. It is non-negotiable.

Don't just pray because you are in trouble, make it your lifestyle to remain in touch with God through prayer, without ceasing.

Prayer

Dear Lord Jesus, thank You for showing me the way to the Father. You stayed connected to heaven throughout Your stay here on earth, always praying and seeking the Father's will.

I receive the grace to be an effective praying Christian. Help me to exercise self-control over my flesh so that, I do not become enslaved to its weaknesses. I declare according to Your word that, I am strong, my prayer life is vibrant and my relationship with you is satisfyingly fulfilling. I am your child!

NOTES

Ten

The Role of the Holy Spirit in Prayer

10

THE ROLE OF THE HOLY SPIRIT IN PRAYER

The ministry of the Holy Spirit is greatly needed in today's church. Jesus called Him the Spirit of Truth who would guide us into all truth (John 16:13). If you want to know the truth, get to know the Person of the Holy Spirit.

He helps us to pray the mind of God into existence. Many times, we pray amiss because we have no idea how to pray effectively about a particular situation. But when the Holy Spirit is involved, He leads us to pray right. Why? Because He knows the mind of God, He knows the will of God concerning the situation you are presenting and when you connect with Him in prayer, He takes hold with you to pray according to God's will; Romans 8:27:

"Now He who searches the hearts knows what the mind of the Spirit

is, because He makes intercession for the saints according to the will of God."

Praying in tongues & prayer: This is a very important subject that must be taught and encouraged in every Bible believing church.

Why do we run away from it and avoid talking about it? The Lord Jesus Christ clearly said that, it would be one of the signs that would follow those that believe (Mark 16:17).

The early church witnessed the baptism of the Holy Spirit and they spoke with new tongues and tremendous things happened. Peter who out of fear betrayed Jesus became so bold after that experience, he preached and thousands came to Christ.

Acts 2:4 says: *"And they were all filled with the Holy Spirit and began to speak with other tongues, as the Spirit gave them utterance."* Clearly one of the evidences that, a believer is filled with the Holy Spirit is through speaking with new tongues. It is a divine ability one should embrace with no reservation, Paul encourages this (1Corinthians 14:14-15).

The Holy Spirit helps us to pray the will of God when we pray because in our understanding we are limited. You can only pray for so long in your understanding but when you key into the spirit, and begin to pray in tongues concerning a situation as the Holy Spirit gives you utterance, you pray mysteries into existence. Romans 8:26 says: *"Likewise the Spirit also helps in our weaknesses. For we do not know what we should pray for as we ought, but the Spirit Himself makes intercession for us with groanings which cannot be uttered."* Amplified translation says: **"groanings too deep for words,"** the Holy Spirit enables us to do that. This is a great privilege God has extended to us freely.

The Holy Spirit begins to live in the heart of a believer as soon as he/she gets born again. As Jesus said before He left this world, the Holy Spirit is your Teacher, your Helper, your Guide and so on, (John 14:6;26). He speaks to you if you listen to Him and He will convict you when you do something wrong, so that, you can make it right with God. He convicts hearts, He does not condemn (John 16:8).

However, the ability to speak in tongues is a free gift given by the Lord, to all who will receive it and allow the Holy Spirit to flow through them.

You get filled with the Holy Spirit by asking the Lord, you speak in tongues by simply yielding yourself to the Spirit, and allowing Him to take hold of your faculty for this beautiful language to flow through you (Luke 11:11-13). Trying to figure it out with your natural mind will not help you, speak and watch Him express Himself through you. It is an amazing free gift to all believers.

There are times when something is impressed on your heart, and you cannot figure it out in your understanding; you may have a foreboding of some sort regarding a situation or someone, and your understanding is limited to interpret it. You can ask the Holy Spirit to help you pray the will of God concerning the situation or the person, when you pray in the spirit.

In such a case, when you have prayed adequately enough, you will experience a sense of relief and peace regarding the person or the situation. Though you have just prayed in an unknown tongue, the Holy Spirit has taken hold with you to take care of the situation.

In many cases, when you pray in the spirit, you will find yourself switching back into praying in your understanding, speaking the interpretation of your tongues in prayer. Paul admonishes us to pray that, we may interpret the tongues we speak (1Corinthians 14:13).

Don't wait any longer, if you are not experiencing this yet, ask God to fill you and ask the Holy Spirit to give you utterance and start using it.

In a church service setting, when one prophesies through speaking in tongues, scripturally speaking, there should be an interpretation so that all may be edified (1Corinthians 14:26-27).

If you are already speaking in tongues, I encourage you to utilize it fully because you will be edifying yourself, building up your most holy faith every time, Jude 1:20 says: *"But you beloved, building yourselves up on your most holy faith, praying in the Holy Spirit."*

Remember, we are faced with many issues in life that we can't adequately articulate in words, but when we take these things to God in prayer and allow the Holy Spirit to help us, we will receive answers to our prayers, in accordance with God's will for those situations.

Prayer

Dear Holy Spirit, thank You for Your ministry that is full of power, enabling me to live life victoriously through Christ Jesus. I receive a fresh dose of your anointing daily, to help me carry out the divine assignments that have been given to me.

Fill me anew to the overflow and refresh me.

Help me to know You more and more, and let me become intimately acquainted with You so that, I might know and walk in God's perfect will for me in Jesus' name.

NOTES

Eleven

Prayer as a Boundary Against satanic Plans and Forces

11

PRAYER AS A BOUNDARY AGAINST SATANIC PLANS AND FORCES

The role of prayer in destroying the plans of the enemy cannot be over emphasized. We live in a very chaotic world right now and fear is all around. It looks like the enemy is running rampage, so many people are turning to the wrong systems for solutions. If only believers would pray!

The people of old demonstrated this and averted many plans of the enemy. Prayer always sets a boundary against demonic activities and satanic attacks. The enemy wanted to take Peter out but Christ prayed for him so that his faith would not fail. His prayer created a boundary to how far Peter could go after he betrayed Christ (Luke 22:31-32).

King Herod killed James the brother of John, the church was alive but did not do much then. The same Herod seized Peter to kill him also, the church woke up to pray and prayed until something happened! Peter was rescued by God's angel. What if the church did not pray? Peter would have also been killed by Herod (Acts 12:5-17).

These things show clearly that, some things will not happen until we pray, either in our personal lives or corporately. Some things will also happen when we pray. Prayer is a powerful way to curb the tactics of the enemy because he is always at work. 1Peter 5:8 says: *Be sober, be vigilant, because your adversary the devil walks about like a roaring lion seeking whom he may devour."*

Christ has given us authority over every ability of the enemy, but it is up to us to rise up and exercise that authority (Luke 10:19). He has done His part, now it is our turn to do our part.

When the apostles were threatened and told not to speak in the name of Jesus anymore, they did not go and hide somewhere, rather they got other believers together and prayed. The Bible says in Acts 4:31 that: *"And when they had prayed, the place where they were assembled was shaken; and they were all filled with the Holy Spirit, and they spoke the word of God with boldness."* **Prayer** did this for them, it kept the enemy at bay, and gave them the boldness they needed, to keep doing the assignment the Master gave them. If only we would pray!

Prayer

Father in the powerful Name of the Lord Jesus, Your word says that, we wrestle not against flesh and blood but against principalities and powers, rulers of darkness and spiritual wickedness in high places. I take authority over every force of darkness sent against me, my destiny, my loved ones and the purpose of God for our lives. I render all their abilities useless and of no effect in the mighty name of Jesus' Christ.

I declare and decree victory over every situation at war against me and mine. I speak life over every circumstance and I declare that we are overcomers in Jesus' name.

Hallelujah! We have been redeemed from every curse through Him who loved us and died for us. In Jesus' name I claim our deliverance. Amen.

NOTES

Twelve

Hindrances to Effective Prayer

12

HINDRANCES TO EFFECTIVE PRAYER

Prayer is a powerful tool in the life of any believer but as powerful as it is, it can also be hindered. Many prayers are not getting their desired results because there are obstacles hindering them. Let us examine a few of these hindrances.

1. **Unforgiveness:** This is a major hindrance to prayer but unfortunately many believers are not aware of this, they pray day and night and harbor unforgiveness in their hearts. Their prayers are not answered and they wonder why.

    Mark 11:25 says: *"And whenever you stand praying, if you have anything against anyone, forgive him, that your Father in heaven may also forgive you your trespasses."*

26. "But if you do not forgive, neither will your Father in heaven forgive your trespasses."

It is clearly written in these verses of scripture that, as loving as God is, if we have unforgiveness in our hearts towards others, God will not also forgive us our sins, and if this is the situation, how can our prayers be answered?

You may be reading this, and you may be dealing with unforgiveness in your heart, maybe you find it difficult to forgive and let go, I want to encourage you to receive the enabling grace of God. This will help you to forgive where you have found it hard to do so. As it is commonly said that, "unforgiveness is a prison" if you toy with it, you are keeping yourself imprisoned. Receive God's grace today to forgive things done against you, release others from those offenses and receive your own freedom.

2. **Doubt:** Another major hindrance to prayer is doubt. The Bible says in James 1:6-7: *"But let him ask in faith, with no doubting, for he who doubts is*

like a wave of the sea driven and tossed by the wind. 7. "For let not that man suppose that, he will receive ANYTHING from the Lord."

What an eye opener to know that, coming to God with doubt in one's heart could be a hindrance to prayers! We must have total confidence in God's ability and this comes by believing that, He is who He says He is in His word, no questions asked. Take Him at His word. A doubtful person is one who is doubleminded, that is, wavering and undecided or having two opinions (James 1:6-8). To win the war over this, is to trust Him wholly even when it doesn't make sense to the natural mind.

3. **Unbelief:** The state of a heart that deals with unbelief is (1) one that refuses to accept that God is and can do what He says He can do; OR (2) believes that God can do anything but doubts if, God will intervene in a particular situation. Unbelief and doubt are not the same, in the sense that, a doubting person is questioning truth, he/she may be seeking answers or evidence but an unbelieving heart is not

accepting the truth. Neither of these is better than the other but the cure to both is similar.

Get out of the realm of sense in your mind, the realm that tries to analyze God. Take Him at His word, judge Him faithful like the Bible says of Sarah in Hebrews 11:11: *"By faith Sarah herself also received strength to conceive seed, and she bore a child when she was past the age, because she judged Him faithful who had promised."*

4. **Praying outside of God's will**: God's will is His word and He will never contradict Himself, so if you want to receive answers to your prayers, those prayers must be in line with His will. The Bible says this in 1John 5:14: *"Now this is the confidence that we have in Him, that if we ask anything according to His will, He hears us."* Since this is so, then praying outside of His will does not get answers.

To know what His word says is to know His will. If you have a situation, find out what the word of God says concerning that situation and take it to God in prayer and declare it verbally. This is how to pray in line with His will and get His attention.

5. **Fear**: This is another major hindrance to prayer because it can literally stop you in your tracks. It is often said that: "fear is the opposite of faith" and the Bible says in Hebrew 11:6 that: *"But without faith, it is impossible to please Him for he who comes to God must believe that He is, and that, He is a Rewarder of those who diligently seek Him."*

To stop fear, feed your faith and exercise it. You feed your faith by studying and meditating in the word of God. Say what the word says, believe it and the voice of fear will be drowned, and faith will rise in your heart. To harbor fear is to walk in doubt and unbelief, they work hand in hand. Get in to the word of God and get rid of fear so that, faith can take its rightful position in your heart, and you can receive answers to your prayers.

6. **Negative confession**: I cannot over emphasize how saying what the enemy wants you to say, can be a hindrance to

your prayers. Faith is agreeing with God's word and when you agree with something, you not only believe it, you also declare it. The Bible says in Proverbs 18:21 that: *"Death and life are in the power of the tongue, and those who love it will eat its fruit."* What we say in prayer if it's God's will, must also be what we confess with our mouth. This does not mean you should be in denial of the situation you may be going through, it simply means, you get on the side of the word of God concerning your situation. While what you are going through may be a fact, the word of God is the truth and it always overtakes the fact.

When you have prayed in line with God's will, stay on that platform of faith, because it is the guarantee for your victory. Consistently declare what His will is, speak the word! Saying anything negative about what you are trusting God for, negates your prayer and kills it completely. The answer is to keep releasing life by declaring what the word of God says concerning the situation.

7. **Worry:** As simple as it sounds, it is a huge hindrance to prayer. Worry does nothing

good for the soul, the body or prayers. The Lord once showed me a picture of what worry means to prayer. It means when you pray, leave it in God's hands and trust Him. However, the moment you start worrying about it after you have prayed, you have taken your request back from God and He has nothing to work with!

How do you deal with worry? DON'T! Worry not! Fret not! When you take anything to God in prayer, leave it in His hands. The Bible says in Philippians 4:6-7: *"Do not be anxious about anything, but in everything by prayer and supplication with thanksgiving, let your requests be made known to God. And the peace of God, which surpasses all understanding, will guard your hearts and your minds through Christ Jesus."* PRAY, DON'T WORRY!

8. **Sin:** The issue of sin is not always what many people want to confront in their lives but it is another hindrance to prayer. The Bible says in Psalm 66:18 that: *"if I regard iniquity in my heart, the Lord will not hear."* This shows clearly that, harboring sin in our hearts can hinder our prayers. Remedy for this is to humble oneself, confess, repent

and forsake those sins. The Bible says in 1John1:8-9: *"If we say that we have no sin, we deceive ourselves, and the truth is not in us. If we confess our sins, He is faithful and just to forgive us our sins, and to cleanse us from all unrighteousness."*

9. **Praying amiss** – Many prayers go unanswered because the motives are wrong. James 4:3 says: *"Ye ask, and receive not, because ye ask amiss, that ye may consume it upon your lusts."* Surely God wants to bless His children but we must pray in line with His purpose and design, not with the wrong motives. Just as one of the points in this chapter suggests, the best way not to pray amiss, is to find out what God has made provision for in His word, as it relates to your situation and pray in line with it.

10. **Disobedience:** God is a God of principles and we must respect His principles. Breaking those principles while still expecting prayers to be heard will not work. For example, if you are not faithful to Him in giving as required in His word, you are in direct disobedience to that particular principle. Praying for a financial

breakthrough in that regard is like a joke. His word says that, when we do not tithe, we rob Him, the same word also says, He will rebuke the devourer for our sakes when we do tithe (Malachi 3:10-12). In order to enjoy that benefit, the principle of giving must be obeyed. This applies to every principle of God in His word, prayers will be hindered when disobedience is at play.

Prayer

Dear Lord, thank You for all your love, kindness and mercy. I receive the grace to keep my heart pure at all times, devoid of everything that can hinder my prayers and relationship with you.

I receive the grace not to play into the hands of the enemy nor dwell on negative situations when they arise. I keep my spiritual pipeline unclogged so that, Your Holy Spirit can freely flow in and through me. Help me to live a life that is pleasing to you in Jesus' name.

NOTES

Thirteen

Prayer and Fasting

13

PRAYER AND FASTING

Prayer as important as it is, can also be enhanced through fasting. However, there have been many misconceptions about fasting, which have made many people shun the idea of participating in the exercise.

To fast is to willingly abstain from food or drink for a chosen period of time, for a particular purpose in prayer. In today's world, fasting will simply mean abstinence from (apart from food or drink) whatever activity one chooses for a period of time. Many people fast social media, games, television and some other habits that consume their attention.

To describe fasting in my own way, is to say that: "It is the purpose of shutting down the flesh through abstinence from food for a specific period of time; avoiding distractions, so that, one's spirit can be more in tune with the Holy Spirit; doing this, with a purpose and focused determination to seek the face of God in prayer."

We do not fast to manipulate God because He cannot be manipulated, it is for our own benefits. Our flesh many times gets in the way, it rules our mind, will and emotions. One effective way of keeping the flesh in check is through fasting.

Fasting helps our prayer to be more effective, in that, we are able to hear God more because our spirit man is alert since the flesh has been subdued.

Coupling fasting with prayer once in a while is essential for a believer, it will bring about much spiritual growth and deeper walk with God. Jesus told His disciples when they could not cast out a demon in a particular case. They asked him why they couldn't do it and His response is shown in Matthew 17:21: *"However, this kind does not go out except by prayer and fasting."* This clearly shows that, in order to operate in some levels of anointing, fasting must accompany a consistent prayer life.

This is not a book about fasting but let us examine some types of fast that, we as believers can engage in to enrich our lives spiritually.

Dry Fast – This is total abstinence from both food and drink for a period of time, mostly 24 hours or more. This is seen also in the book of Esther 4:16. Esther summoned a 3-day dry fast to seek God's divine intervention for herself and country.

Liquid only fast – This is carried out by avoiding foods and taking only liquids for a chosen period. Some people drink only water, while others drink juices or smoothies. The Lord Jesus went without food for 40 days and 40 nights. Matthew 4:2: *"After He had gone without food for forty days and forty nights, He became hungry."*

Partial fast – This comes in different forms depending on individuals. One may eat a meal a day, preferably dinner while skipping breakfast and lunch. Some may only skip breakfast. Some abstain from certain types of food and drink for a period of time.

The popular Daniel fast comes under this category as well. The Bible tells us that, Daniel and his friends determined not to eat the king's meat and drink his wine so as not to defile themselves. As a result of this, Daniel and his friends requested only vegetables and water, Daniel 1:12 says: *"Please, test your servants for ten days and let us be given some vegetables to eat and water to drink."* This was where the term "Daniel fast" originated from.

When a believer engages in a fast, it must have a targeted purpose, if not, it is as good as going on a hunger strike with no results. Prayer and fasting coupled together will produce dynamic results. We humble ourselves before God when we fast to seek His face, this enlarges our spiritual capacity and keeps us disciplined to hear Him more clearly.

NOTES

CONCLUSION

I truly pray that, this book has widened your horizon spiritually in one way or another. As you must have noticed, it is a book full of practical terms, so I want to encourage you not only to read it but to also do what it says and teach it to others as well. I believe that, the anointing of God rests upon the content of the book and by the help of the Holy Spirit, it is transferred to the reader and power is released.

It has been my joy to be a vessel and a carrier of God's message. Now that you have been blessed, please pass the blessing on to someone else.

For group Bible studies, there are worksheets available for free download, please contact our office through the website at www.toyinjohn.com to be sent the link.

In Christ's love!

Toyin John

"The heartfelt and persistent prayer of a righteous man (believer) can accomplish much when put into action and made effective by God, it is dynamic and can have tremendous power." James 5:16b (Amplified)

TO CONTACT THE AUTHOR

To know more about Toyin or to invite her to speak at your church or events and conferences, you may contact her office through her personal website at www.toyinjohn.com.

To send your prayer requests, please fill out a prayer request form on the prayer ministry's website at www.pushprayer.org. The prayer team attends to every request.

Follow Toyin John on Twitter #toyinspeakslife, Instagram @toyinspeakslife and Facebook.

For inspirational message videos, you may subscribe to her YouTube channel on YouTube.

Toyin John is a Certified Speaker, Coach and Trainer with the John Maxwell Team. She is the Founder of Giant Within LLC, a Coaching and Consulting firm that is dedicated to helping organizations as well as individuals reach their peak performance. For group or one-on-one coaching & training services, please contact her through her personal website at www.toyinjohn.com.

Another book available by Toyin John both in print and kindle version on Amazon.com and in print only at www.toyinjohn.com.

Made in the USA
San Bernardino, CA
05 September 2017